THE KINGDOM OF HEAVEN

SIX YOUTH GROUP STUDIES FROM

MATTHEW

ROGER FAWCETT

CF4·K

10 9 8 7 6 5 4 3 2 1

ISBN: 978-1-84550-643-8
© 2011 Roger Fawcett
Edited by David Jackman and Thalia Blundell

Published in 2011 by
Christian Focus Publications, Geanies House, Fearn,
Tain, Ross-shire, IV20 1TW, Great Britain.
www.christianfocus.com
Cover design by Paul Lewis
Printed by Bell and Bain, Glasgow

Scripture quotations used in this book are from the Holy Bible, New
International Version. Copyright © 1973, 1978, 1984, International
Bible Society. Used by permission of Zondervan Bible Publishers.

CONTENTS

INTRODUCTION

BY NICK MARGESSON

As a youth leader you have the great privilege of introducing young people to the Lord Jesus Christ and helping them to grow in the Christian faith. The 14-18s age group are at the junction between the younger teens and the adult church and this is often where we lose them. *The Junction* is a series of books designed to help you teach older teens to study the Bible in a way which is challenging and intellectually stretching. Because they are often unprepared to take things at face value and are encouraged to question everything, it is important to satisfy the mind while touching the heart. The ready-to-use sessions contained in the books are for youth groups of varying sizes, with normal leaders and normal teenagers who want to serve an awesome God.

Each book in the series contains one teaching module, which will normally last from 4-7 weeks. At the front of the book is an overview of the Bible teaching, which can be photocopied for your church leader so that he/she is aware of what is being taught. Each lesson plan, in addition to a lesson aim, contains study notes to enable the leader to understand the Bible passage, a slot to encourage the young people to share experiences and learn from each other, a suggestion to focus attention on the study to follow, suggestions for a prayer and praise time and an optional worksheet to help the young people engage with the passage. Recognising that youth groups vary in size and available space, every effort has been made to include activities that are easily adaptable.

Putting Together a Youth Group Session

What should we include in our youth group sessions?

If you wander into any Christian bookshop and ask the question, 'What should we include in our youth group sessions?' you had better be prepared for a very long stay in the bookshop! Just about every book on youth ministry that you pick up off the shelf will give you a different answer to that question – generally based on the author's preference, upbringing, experiences, etc. Interestingly, if you pick up your Bible and ask the same question you will also be in for a long wait, because, as far as I can see, the Bible never mentions youth groups, let alone what might be involved in a youth group session. In fact, the Bible very rarely makes any distinction between particular groupings of Christians – it talks about all Christians and makes no particular distinction about age or nationality or background, etc.

So, if our youth group is a Christian youth group, then the question we really need to ask is, 'What does it look like when Christians (of any age) get together?' And, on this subject, the Bible has plenty to say! One of the most complete descriptions of what this looks like in practice comes in Acts 2:42-47, where we are given a fairly detailed description of what the earliest group of believers was like. Whenever God's people got together, they engaged in a whole variety of activities – they prayed together, they praised God together, they learned from God's word together, they reminded each other of what God had done for them, they cared practically for each other, they spent plenty of time together, they cared for the world around them, they proclaimed the good news of Jesus, and so on. You

could sum it up by saying that they were devoted to God and devoted to each other. And, interestingly, this type of devotion was clearly very attractive to the world around them – 'the Lord added to their number daily those who were being saved' (Acts 2:47).

If our youth group is a Christian youth group then, in a youth appropriate way, we need to be displaying that same devotion to God and to each other whenever we meet together. What elements in our youth group sessions will help our groups to do this?

- **Time** – it is noticeable in Acts 2 how much time the early believers spent together. They met together daily in the temple courts, they ate together, they hung out at each other's homes.

    With busy teenagers and busy leaders, spending this much time together would be impossible for just about every youth group, but relationships are a key element of being devoted to one another, and relationships need time and space to develop. In our programming we need to allow time and space for young people and leaders to hang out together.

    Food is a great way to get people to spend time together and, again, it does not have to be complicated or fancy – a bag of doughnuts or some cheese toasties or a pizza are not difficult to arrange.

    In the session outlines in this material, we have not included hang-out time because the way it works best will be different for each group. The hang-out time does not have to be particularly structured but it does need to happen.

- **Teaching** – in Acts 2 we are told that the believers devoted themselves to the apostles' teaching (verse 42). The apostles were commissioned by Jesus to be the authoritative teachers of the early church (John 15:26-27). In the New Testament, the apostles' teaching is authenticated as God's word through signs and wonders (Acts 2:43).

Of course, today, we have the amazing privilege of being able to listen to the apostles' teaching and so listen to God's word whenever the Bible is opened and read and studied. Being devoted to God must, at least, mean listening to his word and trying to put it into practice in our lives. This is why really good Bible teaching needs to be at the centre of our youth group sessions.

In the session outlines in this material, the 'Bible Time' is one of the key elements to the session. There will usually be a couple of components to the 'Bible Time' – an introductory Bible activity (Focus) followed by a short Bible study.

For more help on teaching the Bible to young people, please see 'Seven Top Tips for Teaching the Bible to Young People' on page 10.

- **Sharing and Testimony** – one of the ways that Christians show that they are devoted to one another is by getting to know one another and by listening and learning from each other. In our youth group sessions it is great to be able to programme in times where people can get to know each other a bit better. That might be by running a simple mixer activity or by interviewing somebody or by asking people to share their experiences or thoughts on a particular topic or issue.

In the session outlines in this material we have included a 'Talk Time' in each session. Sometimes these 'Talk Times' are specifically linked to the teaching topic for that session and sometimes they just refer to general issues facing Christians.

We have also included an optional 'Getting to Know You' slot in each session. If your group members already know each other really well then you may decide that this activity is unnecessary.

- **Prayer** – One of the most foundational activities that Christians engage in when they meet together is prayer. Prayer reflects our common status as forgiven sinners who are dependent on God. Prayer demonstrates our concern for and commitment to one another. And yet prayer is often one of the first things that gets dropped from a youth group session or from the programme generally – usually because praying together is embarrassing or hard work. If our groups are Christian groups then we need to pray together and for one another. In fact, although it can be hard work getting a group praying, one of the best ways to grow in devotion to one another is by praying together.

  In the session outlines in this material we have included a 'Prayer Time' in each session. Sometimes this prayer time is directed and flows out of the Bible teaching; sometimes the prayer time is more general.

- **Praising God** – right at the heart of what it means to be Christian, both individually and corporately, is praising God. The psalmist overflows with praise to God, so do the early Christians in Acts 2, and so should the young people in our youth groups.

  Whenever young people meet together as Christians, they ought to be reminded of what God has done and encouraged to praise him. This may mean singing together, but for groups that would prefer not to sing, it will mean exploring other ways to express praise to God – perhaps in reading a Psalm together.

In the session outlines in this material we have included a 'Praise Time' in every session, and have made suggestions for both musical and non-musical youth groups.

- **Practical Care** – probably the most striking and challenging aspect of the early believers' life together, as described in Acts 2, is the practical care that they show for one another: 'All the believers were together and had everything in common. Selling their possessions and goods, they gave to anyone as he had need.'

This practical and material care for each other ought to be reflected in all Christian youth groups, but rarely seems to be (in the western world at least). We need to give serious thought to how we care for one another practically and how that expresses itself in a youth group environment.

In the session outlines in this material, we have not included suggestions for practical care because the way it works best will be different for each group, but practical care is an important part of what it means to be Christians together and we need to make sure that it is happening in our groups.

Seven Top Tips for Teaching the Bible to Young People

Tip 1 – Pray

It is God's word that we are teaching so we need his help to teach it. Ultimately, he is the only one who can open our eyes to understand the Bible and open the eyes of the young people in our youth groups. So we need to pray when we are preparing, and while we are teaching and afterwards, that God would be at work through the Holy Spirit, helping people to listen, understand and put into practice what we are hearing from God's word.

Tip 2 – The Bible must set the agenda

If we are going to teach the Bible properly to young people we need to let the Bible do the teaching. We need to make sure that what we are teaching in a youth group session is what the passage teaches, and not what we, as the leaders, want to teach or what we think the young people need to hear.

Obviously, as we have planned the programme or picked the topics, we will have had some ideas about why we are teaching that particular topic, but when it actually comes down to dealing with the passage, we need to teach what it says and not what we want it to say. And we need to make sure that all of the elements that go to make up a youth group session work together in teaching the passage.

Tip 3 – Be clear without compromising

The key to good communication is clarity – see Nehemiah 8:8. And the key to clarity is knowing what you want to teach and working out how to teach it in a way that is appropriate, understandable and memorable.

Please note: teaching clearly is not the same as being simplistic or dumbing-down; even the most difficult or complicated truths can be taught to young people if they are taught clearly. Inevitably this means that a good amount of work needs to be done in preparation to make sure that you, as the teacher, understand a passage or a topic. After all, if we do not understand a passage or a topic clearly, then what hope do we have of teaching it clearly to others?

Having done the hard work of understanding a passage or topic, we need then to think carefully about how we communicate that to our target audience. It is a useful exercise to ask whether we are teaching in a way that is appropriate, understandable and memorable.

Tip 4 – Good relationships help good teaching

It is generally true to say that good relationships facilitate good communication – see I Thessalonians 2:8. Of course, it is possible to communicate perfectly effectively with a complete stranger, but it is fair to say that, in normal circumstances, communication is easier where there is a good relationship in place. For instance, in trying to work out what level of communication is appropriate (see above) it helps to know the young people with whom we are trying to communicate, particularly in terms of language, illustration and application.

Some things to remember about developing relationships with young people:

• Make the Effort

Building relationships with young people takes time and effort, so we need to make sure that there is enough space in our programme for relationships to develop.

• Make Boundaries

Relationships flourish where there are clear and consistently enforced boundaries. It is possible to fall into the trap of thinking that being friends with a young person means allowing them to do what they like or never telling them off. Adult friendships do not work like that and neither do relationships between adults and young people. Young people need to know 'where they stand'; they need to feel secure in relationships and sometimes that means being firm in terms of discipline, boundaries, etc.

• Be Yourself

Young people want to relate to adults, so be yourself and do not try to be a teenager. Young people have plenty of friends of their own age, but what many are looking for, particularly in the transition between child and adult, is adults who will value and take an interest in them. Many teenagers, particularly if they are going through a period of conflict or non-communication with their parents, will look for supportive relationships with other adults. Interestingly, this relationship is often developed with a grandparent.

This means that youth and children's leaders do not have to pretend to be younger than they are. It also means that when we are putting together teams to work with children and young people, we do not have to limit ourselves to young leaders.

• Listen

Genuine relationships are two-way. So, in building relationships with young people, we need to listen and be appropriately honest and open. Paul talks about sharing his life with the Thessalonians (1 Thessalonians 2:8).

• Do not take yourself too seriously!

Because relationships are two-way, there is a possibility that we, as leaders, will be let down in a relationship. This is often the case with teenagers, who may not attach the same importance and significance to a relationship, so it is important that adult leaders do not take themselves too seriously.

Tip 5 – Be aware of the culture but not a slave to it

There is a school of thought that says that those who are involved in youth and children's work have to immerse themselves in the culture of young people – live how they live, dress how they dress, do what they do, etc. That is NOT what is being suggested here. Quite apart from anything else, youth culture is extremely difficult to define, partly because it is a mixture of all sorts of cultures and partly because no young person willingly fits into the 'typical' category.

There are, however, clearly differences between the world of young people and the world of adults. But, as we have seen already, young people want to relate to adults, and are therefore expecting that there will be a degree of cultural diversity. In fact, it is often this cultural diversity which adds value to the relationship – the fact that someone from a different world, culturally, is taking an interest in me and my world.

Having said all that, taking an interest in their lives and the world in which they live is an indication that we care for people, so it is worth being aware of the culture of the young people with whom we are working. So we might not like the music that they are into, but we can still ask about it. We may not watch the same programmes that they like, but we can still be aware of them.

In particular, if we are trying to communicate to teenagers, then it is worth learning about communication in the world of young people. Obviously, as we spend time with young people, we will begin to learn how they communicate.

However, there are a couple of ways that you can short-cut the process:

- Talk to schoolteachers. They are the ones who are specifically trained to communicate to young people. Good schoolteachers will have a wealth of knowledge and experience in communicating to teenagers.
- Watch television – particularly early in the evening, when programming and advertising is aimed specifically at young people. It is worth watching the advertisements every now and again, because advertisers know how to communicate to teenagers.

Tip 6 – Be varied in communication

One of the lessons from the culture of young people is the need to use variety in our communication. A very quick look at the advertisements or morning television shows us that young people are used to receiving a great deal of information, very quickly. And that information comes in a variety of forms – images, noises, words, instructions, actions, etc. Being varied in communication recognises, as we have seen already, that people learn or take in information differently.

Of course, the Bible itself is full of variety in communication. Sometimes the communication is very visual – dreams, visions, parables or exciting narrative. Even as we read the passages, we are encouraged to visualise what is happening. Sometimes the communication is audible – the prophet speaks, the letter is read out, Jesus talks to somebody – and, again, even as we read these passages, it is as though we are listening in to what is being said. Sometimes the communication in the Bible is more physical – animal sacrifice, Jesus touching the leper, Thomas touching Jesus' hands and side, all communicating theological truth physically.

When teaching the Bible to young people it is important that we allow the richness and diversity of the Bible to be reflected in our teaching.

Tip 7 – Preparation is everything

Preparing a youth group session can be harder than preparing a talk or a study for adults. As well as doing all of the same preparation in terms of understanding the passage, you then have to work out how on earth you are going to communicate it to 14, 16, or 18 year olds.

The more time that leaders are able to take in preparing sessions, the better able they will be to teach young people effectively.

SERIES OVERVIEW
THE KINGDOM OF HEAVEN

Matthew's gospel is the longest of all the gospels in number of chapters and is, therefore, a big undertaking to try and study all at once. However, it is undoubtedly a good thing to aim to get to know one gospel really well and groups are encouraged to do this, if at all possible. As it is impractical to do this in the course of a short series in a book such as this, an appendix has been added to give a starting point for taking each section further.

Matthew was one of Jesus' disciples (9:9-13; 10:1-4) and wrote his gospel with Jewish readers in mind. He starts with a genealogy to show that Jesus was legally descended from Abraham and David and links the Old Testament closely to the New, demonstrating that Jesus is the fulfilment of OT prophecy, e.g. 1:23; 2:18; 2:23; 4:15f; 8:17; 12:18ff; 13:35; 21:5; 27:9f. A major theme is the kingly rule of Jesus and events are recorded as happening in the way they did because God had willed it so.

Matthew constructed his gospel very carefully. One of the ways he did this was to include five major sections covering different aspects of Jesus' teaching. They are easy to spot because each one ends with a 'marker' verse saying something like: 'When Jesus had finished saying these things ...' (see 7:28; 11:1; 13:53; 19:1; 26:1). Matthew also helps us understand the chunks between the five 'discourses' by giving us his own commentary from time to time, e.g. 4:23 and 9:35 are matching bookends, both stating that Jesus travels throughout Galilee teaching and healing. Between the two we have chapters 5-7 (teaching) and 8-9 (healing).

Teaching Matthew by David Jackman and William Philip (2009, Christian Focus Publications) explains this structure in greater detail, especially in the chapter entitled 'A Map and a Key to Matthew's Gospel'. The book is recommended to all those who want to teach through Matthew.

The Kingdom of heaven

Matthew uses the term 'Kingdom of heaven' where Mark and Luke use 'Kingdom of God'. The Jews did not speak the name of God because it was considered too holy to utter.

Kingdom observations:

- Its scope is primarily dynamic rather than spatial, so it refers to the reign of God rather than a Kingdom with borders.
- It doesn't refer to God's universal sovereignty, but to the people who have eternal life, and there are conditions for entry (5:3; 5:20; 7:21).
- It applies to both the present and the future (now and not yet aspect).
- Obedience is the mark of membership of the Kingdom.

LESSON 1

INTRODUCING THE KING

BIBLE READING

Matthew Chapters 1-4

TEACHING POINT

An overview of Matthew's gospel and an introduction to Jesus, God's promised King.

LEADER'S PREPARATION

This study is divided into two parts. The first part is an overview of Matthew's gospel with a few verses to look up, giving an idea of Matthew's style and themes. It is important and helpful to get a grip on the structure because it is such a long gospel. You may want to challenge the group to be reading the whole of Matthew's gospel as you work through these studies together. (For notes on the structure in Matthew see the Series Overview on page 16)

The second part of this study covers the early part of Jesus' life and the beginning of his ministry. It is important that the young people recognise that Jesus is God's promised King so that they take seriously his teaching about God's Kingdom.

QUESTIONS

Part 1 – an overview of Matthew's gospel.

Look at Matthew 1:1-17. Can you see any names you recognise? Why does Matthew want us to associate the birth of Jesus (1:18 onwards) with some of these names?

Matthew starts his book with an oddity – a list of names. Most people will recognise Abraham, Isaac, Jacob, David and Solomon. Some may also recognise Judah, Rahab, Boaz, Ruth and Jesse from familiar Bible stories. Those who have a good grasp of OT history may also recognise some of the kings like Uzziah, Hezekiah and Josiah.

Starting with a genealogy seems strange to us, but was natural and informative for the original readers. Matthew was embarking on a book about Jesus Christ. The readers needed to know that Jesus was the real Messiah or Christ, that he was properly related to the past heroes of the faith. By starting with a genealogy Matthew is firmly linking Jesus with the patriarchs and particularly with David, the King. He is setting forth the case for the authenticity of Jesus' new Kingdom.

1:17   Strictly speaking, there are not fourteen generations. Certain individuals have been left out. Verse 11 states that Josiah was the father of Jeconiah (Jehoiachin), whereas he was actually his grandfather (2 Kings 23:30-34; 24:6).

Matthew presents it like this to make a point. The Old Testament hangs around these events, the promises made to Abraham, their partial fulfilment and further promises made to David, the disaster of the exile, leading to their final fulfilment in Christ.

Look up 7:28; 11:1; 13:53; 19:1; 26:1. What similarities are there between the verses? What does each verse conclude? Why do you think we get this repetition?

These five verses all conclude a longer teaching section in Matthew's gospel (sometimes called 'discourses' but you could equally say 'sermons'.) Each of the verses says something like: 'when Jesus had finished saying these things'.

The repetition helps us divide Matthew's long gospel into easier chunks. Don't forget that there were no chapter and verse breaks originally. Matthew has used five teaching sections interspersed with narrative about Jesus' other activities, healings, miracles and debates. The five teaching sections will form the structure of the rest of these studies.

Look up 4:17 and 23 and 9:35. What is Jesus described as doing? What word is repeated in each verse and what do you think it means?

In 4:17 Jesus begins his ministry by preaching about the Kingdom of heaven. In 4:23 and 9:35 we read that he goes about doing just that – preaching the good news of the Kingdom and demonstrating what it means by healing people.

The repeated word 'Kingdom' implies an area controlled by a king. Jesus himself is that King and the 'Kingdom of heaven' is his Kingdom (some of the other gospel writers call it the 'Kingdom of God' – see Series Overview). Matthew spends a lot of time telling us about this Kingdom and showing us that Jesus is the rightful King. Understanding this theme helps us see why Matthew writes his gospel the way he does.

Part 2 – Jesus is God's promised King.

Matthew does not record the actual birth of Jesus. He is more interested in showing that Jesus came from God and is the one promised by the prophets.

1:18   He was conceived by the Holy Spirit.

1:20   Joseph is referred to as 'son of David'.

1:21   The name Jesus is the same name as Joshua and means 'Yahweh is salvation'. Matthew wants us to know right at the beginning what kind of saving Jesus has come to do.

1:23   Throughout these passages Matthew is anxious to point his readers to OT passages authenticating Jesus as Messiah. Here he refers to Isaiah 7:14.

1:24-25   Joseph's actions show that he believed that Mary had done nothing wrong and that the child was indeed from the Holy Spirit. In naming the child Joseph is owning him, saying, 'He's mine.' This is how Jesus comes into David's line, despite Joseph not being his biological father. (Mary was also a descendent of David, but 'lines' passed through the male side of a family.)

Jesus is a great king, like David. In Matthew 2:1-12 we read of the coming of the magi. These eastern people were almost certainly Gentiles, who knew something of the Jewish Scriptures and faith. They were given the right instructions from the priests and teachers of the Law – Messiah would be born in David's home town and would follow the pattern of David's line, becoming a great King, but also a shepherd and saviour of the people.

Jesus is a rescuer, like Moses. The story of the magi is followed by the escape to Egypt. Just as Pharaoh gave the order for all Israelite male babies to be killed, Herod gives the order for all male babies in Bethlehem to be killed. But God rescues Jesus, just as he rescued Moses.

2:20   This is almost identical to God's instructions to Moses in Exodus 4:19. Again, Matthew is identifying Jesus with Moses.

Read Matthew 3:1-12. What was John preaching? (3:2) Who came to visit him and what did they do? (3:5-6)

In saying that the Kingdom of heaven is near, John the Baptist is announcing that the rule of God, as foretold by the prophets, is imminent. John the Baptist holds a unique place in Scripture because he bridges the gap between Old Testament and New. He acts in every way like an OT prophet – that's why we get the details of his lifestyle. But he operates in the New Testament as the forerunner to Christ (v.3). In John the old way is seen to be giving way to the new.

The urgent plea from John is to prepare for the new Kingdom that was coming. This was done through repentance. People came to visit from the whole region and they showed their seriousness in accepting his message by confessing their sins and being baptised (a symbol of repentance).

Who is John not pleased to see? Why is he suspicious of these people? What does John warn of? (3:7-10)

It seems that the Pharisees and Sadducees, two powerful groups of religious leaders, have come to John, too. They may just have been coming to see what all the fuss was about. They would not have seen the necessity for repenting because they kept the Law perfectly in their own eyes. In fact, the Pharisees interpreted the Law for everybody else. But John is suspicious of these visitors because their lives show no fruit of living according to the Kingdom.

John then warns that the judgment is coming. Trees not producing good fruit will be destroyed. The hint is that the religious leaders will not like what is coming along in the new Kingdom; their authority and authenticity will be challenged. There will be many interchanges between Jesus and the religious leaders in Matthew's book. The tree/fruit idea occurs several times in Matthew (e.g. 7:15 ff; 12:33).

How does John describe Jesus? Why do you think he uses such strong language?

Jesus will be more powerful than John and will baptise, not with water, but with the Holy Spirit. Under the old covenant, the Holy Spirit only came upon certain individuals to enable them to fulfil certain roles. This is a fulfilment of the promise God gave through the prophet Joel, that God would pour out his spirit on all people.

Jesus comes also as a judge (v.12). John's language is strong because the message is important. This is the turning of the age, the beginning of the new Kingdom of heaven. John would certainly have emphasised the imminent judgment aspect of Jesus' ministry because that was in line with his own message of preparing the way and making straight paths for the Lord.

Read 4:17. What is Jesus' message?

Jesus' message is the same as John's – repent, for the Kingdom of heaven is near. The Kingdom of heaven is going to feature much in Jesus' teaching throughout Matthew.

Think. Are you ready to come face to face with Jesus? What do you need to repent of before God's Kingdom arrives in full? What do you think 'fruit in keeping with repentance' might mean for you?

This question is designed to get people thinking about themselves. You can interpret it in two ways. Are you prepared to meet Jesus in the words of Matthew's gospel? Matthew will bring us face to face with Christ and his sometimes difficult teaching – we need to be ready for change. But the wider question is also relevant. Are we ready for the final judgment/harvest? Perhaps we need to find out more about Jesus in order to be prepared.

Welcome

- Introduce yourselves.
- Start the meeting with prayer.

Getting to Know You

What's your favourite book? Give everyone a chance to choose a favourite book and then go round asking everybody in turn. (Note: we know that everybody's favourite book is the Bible, so you could make it the second favourite!) If there is time have people explain a little bit about why they like it. If you have lots of people and very little time, give people some options and let them vote.

Talk Time

Using a large piece of paper, get the young people to write out as much as they can remember from the stories of Jesus' birth without looking in Bibles. How much can we really remember of the Christmas story? Can the groups put everything in order?

Now give each group a pen and ask them to circle the things that occur in Matthew's gospel alone. They can then check their own answers.

Too often our view of the true story of Jesus' birth, ministry and death is a blend of all four gospels. Whilst this is not a terrible thing, we will grow in our knowledge if we begin to sort out which gospel is which. Each gospel has a unique style and aim. Our love for Christ and his work will deepen and our faith will grow as we extend our understanding of his word.

Focus Time

Famous first lines. Find some famous first lines from literary masterpieces and ask people to guess where they come from or to match them to the right book (e.g. 'It was the best of times, it was the worst of times' comes from Dickens, *A Tale of Two Cities*.) If you are stuck, there are websites that will help you.

First lines do become very familiar. It's odd then that Matthew doesn't begin his gospel with a really memorable one like John does.

Bible Time

See the worksheets on pages 82-83 for the Bible Study questions and running order. Photocopy these pages for each group member for use during the study. Before starting the study, make sure that the group members know who Matthew was (9:9-13; 10:1-4).

If you are short of time you might want to summarise the section about Jesus' birth.

Prayer Time

Thank God for sending Jesus. Ask God to help you find out more about God's Kingdom and what it means for you as you study Matthew together for a few weeks.

Praise Time

Praise God for sending Jesus as King. You could sing songs that rejoice in God's Kingdom. If you don't want to sing, read Mary's song from Luke's gospel (Luke 1:46-55) together as you thank God.

Extra Ideas

King for a Day. If you were king or queen for a day, what one rule would you impose? Get the group to draw up a new 'constitution' based on these ideas, e.g. no using mobile phones in public areas, a strict ban on Marmite, etc.

LESSON 2

iNTRODUCiNG THE KiNGDOM

BIBLE READING

Matthew Chapters 5-7

TEACHING POINT

Jesus explains what life in the new Kingdom is like.

LEADER'S PREPARATION

The Sermon on the Mount is a very well known part of the Bible and rightly so, because it provides some very important teaching. To attempt to study it all in one session seems like trying to climb Everest in that short time between afternoon tea and dinner time. It would be absolutely impossible; there are entire sets of studies just on these chapters. If it would help your group to slow down and take in more of the Sermon then feel free to do so. Our aim in this study is to pick out some of the big themes to show how the Sermon on the Mount fits into Matthew as a whole. We will concentrate on 5:1-20 and 7:13-29.

QUESTIONS

Read 4:23-25 What was Jesus doing?

These verses set the scene for chapters 5-7. Jesus is going throughout Galilee preaching 'the good news of the Kingdom' and healing people. Large crowds follow him to listen to his teaching and be healed.

How did this demonstrate that he is the promised King? (Isaiah 35:5-6; 61:1)

These verses were recognised by the Jews as referring to the promised Messiah. Messiah would make the blind see, the deaf hear, the lame walk and the dumb speak. He would also preach good news to the poor.

In 5:1 we read that Jesus, seeing the crowds, goes up a mountain side to teach. He sits down, like a traditional Jewish Rabbi, and begins to teach his disciples, presumably with the crowds pressing in on every side to listen in. (A 'disciple' was a learner, i.e. someone who was following at that moment in time. It does not imply commitment.)

During the 400 years between the end of the Old Testament and the beginning of the New, the teachers of the Law had developed the rabbinic code until it was impossible to keep. The people's lives were bounded by the scribes' interpretation of the Scriptures. Jesus uses the sermon to correct their wrong impressions and beliefs.

Structure of the Sermon – see Information Box (pages 40-41).

Read 5:1-12
What are the Christian characteristics described in these verses? What qualities does the world value rather than these?

Fill in the table:
(Answers supplied but your wording will differ)

Characteristic	Meaning	World's Values
Poor in spirit	Recognising our own spiritual bankruptcy	Self-promotion and DIY spirituality
Those who mourn	Grief over sinfulness	How dare you call me sinful?
Meek	Humble and ready to put others first	Grabbing what you can
Hunger and thirst for righteousness	Considering righteousness as vital	Righteousness an optional extra; life's too busy
Merciful	Compassionate to the helpless (i.e. like us)	I'm not like them, why should I care?
Pure in heart	An inward desire to be holy	It doesn't matter, my inner attitudes affect no one
Peacemakers	Puts ego aside and loves peace for God's sake	My 'rights' come above the need for harmony
Persecuted because of righteousness	Do all of the above and expect a hard time!	Try to avoid being noticed, then you won't suffer

'Blessed' – to be blessed is more than being happy. It means most to be congratulated, to find approval. In the Old Testament the word is used to refer to God's salvation.

The beatitudes are a description of what it means to live under Jesus' kingly rule. They are *not* a list of entry requirements, which is how they are often interpreted.

The second halves of the first and last beatitude are identical (v.3, 10), called inclusion (a stylistic device to show that everything in between follows one theme).

What things stop me living this way? How does it help to know that God is a gracious God?

The Beatitudes describe the norms of the Kingdom, not a list for Christians to pick from. They are not easy reading, but complex and hard-hitting. When teaching this lesson we need constantly to remind ourselves and the group that the characteristics described are not requirements for entry into God's Kingdom, but those to be increasingly displayed by people God has already blessed through the gospel.

It helps to know that God is gracious because we cannot, in this life, achieve the perfect character. We need constantly to approach God for forgiveness. Because God is gracious he will go on forgiving us and slowly changing our character (a process the Bible calls 'sanctification' which means being made holy).

Believers are witnesses for the Kingdom (5:13-16). What two metaphors does Jesus use?

Salt and light are both metaphors to do with Christian witness in the world.

Salt gives flavour and was used as a preservative. Without a Christian presence, the world would become even more rotten.

Light – Christian witness should act as a transforming power in society.

Both salt and light can only have an effect if they are distinctive from their environment yet involved in it. Both are no good if they do not fulfil their function. The righteousness of the life you live attracts attention, even if it is only opposition.

What does Jesus say about his relationship to the Old Testament? (5:17-18)

Jesus fulfilled the Law and the Prophets, (the Jewish Scriptures), because they pointed towards him (v.17). He was also the only one who could keep the Law completely. He had definitely not come to abolish them and did not see himself in opposition to the OT. To understand how Jesus fulfils the OT we need to understand how the OT prophesies (Matthew 11:12-14).

Some prophecies are predictive, looking forward to Messiah, e.g. Micah 5:2. Some are the history of the Jews pointing forward, e.g. Hosea 11:1 refers to the Exodus but is used in Matthew 2:15 to refer to Jesus. The Israelites spent forty years in the desert (Deuteronomy 8) and Jesus spent forty days in the desert (Matthew 4:1-4), where he quoted from Deuteronomy 8:3.

The NT interprets OT verses pointing forward to Christ and the blessings he brings (Hebrews 9:8-10; 10:1-4). So Jesus fulfils the OT Scriptures in many ways and, because they point towards him, he has not come to abolish them.

Jesus is upholding the reliability and truthfulness of the written text. Although in verse 18 he says, 'until heaven and earth disappear', meaning 'never, until the end of time', he qualifies this with 'until everything is accomplished'. Therefore, detailed prescriptions, e.g. food laws, the sacrificial system, (that we do not observe as the Jews did) may well be superseded, because what is prophetic must, in some sense, be provisional.

How do we relate to the Law? (5:19)

Jesus has already fulfilled the Law and made salvation available through God's grace. Our job is to live in obedience to the King, hence Jesus' command to do what he says at the conclusion of the sermon (7:24-27).

The Law and the Prophets prophesy until John the Baptist (Matthew 11:12-14), after which the Kingdom advances. Jesus turns from talking about the Law and prophets to the Kingdom. 'These commandments' is not referring to the OT Law, but to the commands of the Kingdom found in Matthew 5-7.

Christians are not exempt from keeping the Law. The Christian should seek to live in conformity with God's will in gratitude for what God has done in salvation, not to earn his way to heaven. In the remainder of the sermon, Jesus teaches that the proper way to obey God's commands is not through legalistic rule-keeping, but by wanting to please God from the heart.

How can our righteousness surpass that of the Pharisees? (5:20)

The entry requirements for the Kingdom are strict. The Pharisees (so often the 'bad guys') kept the Law meticulously, which would be commendable if it were not just legalistic rule-keeping. The only way the Christian's righteousness can exceed that of the Pharisees is by confessing our spiritual bankruptcy and casting ourselves on God's mercy (see Romans 3:21-24) – there is a righteousness apart from the Law).

Conclusion (7:13-29)

In 5:17 – 7:12 Jesus is explaining the standards required to enter the Kingdom and live as members of it – standards no one can ever reach (5:19-20). The sermon is not telling us what we have to do in order to become members of the heavenly Kingdom, rather, it drives us to God for the grace we need, not just for conversion, but also to live as his people day by day.

Read 7:13-27. What are the four paired alternatives? What does each one teach about following the King?

7:13-14	Two paths
7:15-20	Two trees
7:21-23	Two claims
7:24-27	Two houses

Don't worry if the group uses slightly different wording for the pairs.

Two paths.

There are only two paths. The broad way accommodates many people, is well-travelled, but ends in destruction. The narrow way is found by very few, but ends in life (a synonym for the Kingdom). The significance is not the path itself, but its destination.

God's way is not spacious but confining. Prayer is not easy; righteousness is not easy; achieving transformed, God-centred attitudes is not easy. All these are impossible without God's grace. However, the joy of knowing God through Christ, of Christian friendship, and the liberty of having sins forgiven make the confining aspect seem nothing.

God's way can't be discerned by appeal to majority opinion. We can't travel the narrow road while we are motivated by a desire to please men.

Two trees.

The prophet is a messenger. False prophets appear to be genuine, but they distort the truth. But how can we recognise them? A false prophet doesn't advocate the narrow way of v.13-14. He leaves out the difficult parts of the gospel and his life doesn't match up with Jesus' teaching in chapters 5-7.

Jesus may have been thinking of buckthorn, which had small, black berries easily mistaken for grapes. There was a certain thistle with a flower which, from a distance, could be mistaken for a fig. False prophets, from a certain perspective, can look like true ones, but the nature of their fruit can't be hidden forever. There is an indissoluble link between belief and conduct.

Two claims.

The first group approaches Jesus reverently on judgment day and calls him Lord. Their belief was probably orthodox and they had an impressive record of spiritual experience – prophesying, exorcising demons and performing miracles. Jesus doesn't deny their claims but still calls them evil-doers (those who practise lawlessness).

Genuine disciples are those known to the Lord and who 'know' him (have a relationship with him). Acceptance by God does not depend on what we say or do, but on what Jesus has done on the cross. Obviously, we must also bear in mind that 'faith without works is dead' (James 2:26), so real faith is demonstrated in obedient lives. The essential characteristic of the true believer is obedience to God's will.

Two houses.

The difference between the wise and foolish builders is subtle. Both hear, but only the wise obey what they hear. They put Jesus' words into practice (cf. the fruit of verses 16-20). 'Therefore' (v.24) makes the link to what has gone before. Entrance to the Kingdom depends on obedience, not to earn brownie points, but which bows to Jesus' lordship in everything and without reservation. Such obedience blends with genuine repentance. The focus is on the builders, not the foundations. Only those who do the will of the Father will enter the Kingdom.

Conclusion

There are only two ways. Jesus' way demands repentance, trust and obedience.

Extension Question – How should our thinking be shaped by these exclusive claims in a culture of relativism and pluralism?

Relativism is the idea that truth is something relative to the observer. Your version of truth will be different from mine, and that is okay. We do not have the right (say relativists) to impose our truths on others – there can be no absolute truth. Pluralism is this idea taken into the realm of religion. A pluralist believes that all religions are equally valid and none can claim to be absolutely true at the expense of any other.

Christians have the difficult task of living in a culture where these ideas are instilled from a very early age, yet reconciling this with the claims of the gospel and Christ to be absolute truth. The Sermon on the Mount finishes with several dichotomies, each of which is exclusive in nature. For example, you are either on the broad or narrow path – you cannot be on both at the same time and both cannot be the right path at the same time.

If you choose to discuss this question, use it as an opportunity to challenge the young people's thinking about relativism (which is what will be passively or actively taught in schools). You may not make a lot of headway and many questions will arise, but it is important to help them see that the gospel is the truth and not one alternative amongst many.

PLANNING THE SESSION

Welcome
- Introduce yourselves.
- Start the meeting with prayer.

Getting to Know You

Ask the leaders to think up 2-5 true and false statements about themselves, depending on the number of leaders. The leaders take it in turns to read out their statements. As each one is read out the group has to vote 'true' or 'false' by standing up/sitting down or moving to the appropriate side of the room. The correct answer is announced after each vote. Individual group members keep the score of how many they get right.

At the end of the Sermon on the Mount, Jesus talks about two groups of people, true disciples and false ones. You are either one or the other, just like in the game. Today we're going to find out how to tell them apart.

Talk Time

Sound bites – Find some newspapers with sound bites from politicians and celebrities. Have the young people pick out the sound bites and talk about them. Talk about whether we are turning into a sound bite culture. Ask if anybody can remember any highlights from the Sermon on the Mount. They can use a Bible to see if they recognise anything. Our temptation is to treat the Sermon as a series of sound bites and to cherry-pick the recognisable bits, e.g. 6:33 or 7:7. Unfortunately, children's songs, whilst great for learning verses, encourage this.

However, we need to remember that this is one big teaching block with a theme – life in God's Kingdom – and not a series of sound bites.

Focus Time

Think of ten different occupations, such as fireman, ballet dancer, nurse, banker, chef, etc. Write a description of each one on a separate piece of card and stick them up around the room. e.g. 'I sometimes work through the night, but never leave the station. My engine is red and quite noisy and I am very brave. I'm not afraid of tall buildings, but have to keep quite fit.' (Fireman)

Give each group member a pen and a piece of paper and ask them to guess the occupations. After a set period of time the one with the most right answers wins. Let's see what the Bible has to say about the characteristics of a Christian.

Bible Time

See the worksheets on pages 84-85 for the Bible Study questions and running order. Photocopy these pages for each group member for use during the study.

Start by recapping on a flipchart what we learned about Jesus in the last session:

- descended from Abraham and David (1:1-17)
- came from God and is the one promised by the prophets (1:18-25)
- a great king, like David (2:1-12)
- a rescuer, like Moses (2:13-23)
- the one who will give the Holy Spirit to all believers (3:11)
- the one who will judge (3:12)

i.e. the Messiah, God's promised King.

The amount of detail you can cover in the session will vary. The section from 5:17-20 is vital, because it deals with the way Jesus fulfils the Old Testament, a major theme of Matthew.

Prayer Time

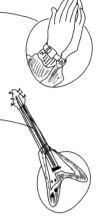

In small groups talk about the things that stop us living God's way. Try to be specific. Pray, thanking God for his grace and asking him for help to live a life pleasing to him in the coming week.

Praise Time

You could sing a song that praises God the Father (6:9), such as 'God of Glory' or 'Our God is an Awesome God'. Or, if your group would enjoy it, you could sing a couple of children's songs like 'The wise man built his house upon the rock'.

If you do not want to sing you could focus on the first two verses of the Lord's Prayer (6:9-10) and talk and pray together about what makes God's name holy. You could read Psalm 111 together, especially thinking about verse 9.

Extra Ideas

To pick up on the idea of the blessings in the Beatitudes, play a game about giving gifts. You could do a Secret Santa (don't worry about what time of year it is). Alternatively the leader could come in with some pictures of presents and everybody could secretly assign the 'gifts' to others in the group. Be as imaginative as you like, e.g. bungee-jumping, season tickets for something, etc. Everybody secretly chooses some presents that they would like to receive. When everybody reveals their choices they score points based on how many 'gifts' they receive that are on their wish list. (This is based on a party game called Gift Trap)

The game reinforces the point that the gifts of the Beatitudes are gifts of grace to the humble. How good God is.

iNFORMATiON BOX
STRUCTURE OF THE SERMON

Introduction (5:1-16)
- The norms of the Kingdom (5:1-12)
- The witness of the Kingdom (5:13-16)

Body of the sermon (5:17 – 7:12)
Bracketed by reference to the Law and the Prophets (5:17; 7:12).
The believer's relationship with the Old Testament Law (5:17-48)
- Jesus is the fulfilment of the Law and the Prophets (OT Scriptures) (v.17-20)
- Six examples of the believer's relationship with the OT Law (v.21-47)
- Conclusion – be perfect, as God is perfect (v.48)

Religious hypocrisy (6:1-18)
- The principle – we should seek God's approval, not men's (v.1)
- Three examples of applying the principle (v.2-18)

Kingdom perspectives (6:19-34)
- Kingdom values (v.19-24)
  Three metaphors:
  - treasure (v.19-21)
    Earthly treasure is anything valuable which is perishable or can be lost.
  - light (v.22-23)
    The good eye is the one fixed on Jesus.
  - slavery (v.24)
    You can only be loyal to one master.

- Don't worry about mere things (v.25-34)
  - general principle (v.25)
    God, who provides important things like life and bodies, will also provide things of lesser importance.
  - Two examples:
    life and food (v.26-27)
    body and clothes (v.28-30).
  - Conclusion (v.31-34)
    Our part is to pursue God's Kingdom.
    God's part is to provide for his children's needs.
    Lack of trust is essentially pagan.

Balance and perfection (7:1-12)
- Three imperatives:
  - do not be judgmental (v.1-5)
  - don't be undiscriminating (v.6)
  - you must persist in the pursuit of God, exercising child-like trust as you do so (v.7-11).
- The golden rule (v.12)
  Do to others what you would have them do to you, not because you want to receive that treatment, but because that sums up the whole of the Law and the Prophets.

Conclusion (7:13-27)
The hearers must make a choice.

Concluding verses (7:28-29)
The response of the crowd – Jesus taught with authority, not like the teachers of the Law.

LESSON 3

PROCLAIMING THE KINGDOM

BIBLE READING

Matthew Chapter 10

TEACHING POINT

Jesus teaches what it means to be a messenger of the gospel.

LEADER'S PREPARATION

When you become a Christian you become a messenger. Joining the Kingdom means automatically becoming the King's ambassador. That is why, towards the beginning of his ministry, Jesus teaches the disciples what it means to be a representative of the King. As you read this chapter notice the emphasis on hardship. It's not easy living God's way and taking Jesus seriously.

We must also realise that there is a difference between things that are relevant just for the disciples, with broad principles for us, and things that will be true for the missionary church down the ages. For example, Jesus sends the disciples to the 'lost sheep of Israel' (10:6), whereas we are not called just to evangelise people with a Jewish background. This instruction to the disciples is superseded by the great commission (Matthew 28:19) and the call to 'all nations'.

Be warned, this is not an easy chapter to digest as it is about true discipleship in the face of opposition from the world. It is not the often taught (but misconstrued) idea that becoming a Christian will make life easy and trouble-free. Chapter 10 is, nonetheless, a great chapter for those struggling with difficulties at school.

QUESTIONS

Read Matthew 9:35 – 10:1. How does Matthew summarise Jesus' ministry so far? What authority does he give to his disciples?

The context for the chapter comes at the end of chapter 9. In chapters 5–9, Matthew has demonstrated Jesus' authority through both his words and his deeds (7:28-29; 8:1-16; 8:23 – 9:8; 9:18-33). Matthew 9:35-38 acts as a summary, ending with the command to his disciples to pray that God will send out workers into his harvest field (v. 38). In 10:1, Jesus prepares to send his own disciples out to do gospel work and the rest of the chapter is the training they receive. It is a huge privilege to read this 'evangelism training' seminar.   *Read 10 v 1 – 16*

What was their target group and what was the message? (10:5-7)

They were sent to the Jews (the 'lost sheep of Israel') and forbidden to go to Samaria and the Gentiles. This is not the case for us (see Leader's Preparation) and alerts us to the fact that not everything in the passage will be directly applicable to our situation.

The message is simple: 'The Kingdom of heaven is near'. It's the gospel. The Kingdom was literally near because Jesus was present and was soon to die on the cross and make the Kingdom available to all. Our own wording might not be the same, but our core message about Jesus the King and the need for people to become members of his Kingdom is just the same.

What tools were the disciples given to authenticate the message? (10:1, 8)

Their mission paralleled Jesus' ministry, including healing as well as preaching (see 4:17 and the miracles recorded in chapters 8-9). Their role as Jesus' messengers and authority to heal, etc., was a free gift, not something they had bought or earned, so must be exercised freely. The continuation of Jesus' ministry by the apostles in Acts was also accompanied by miracles.

The question these verses raise is whether we should expect the same sort of authentication today. Certainly, we hear of such things from time to time and should not rule out any way that God may choose to intervene in our world. A better question to ask is how much we need the same authentication? We have the record of Jesus' and the apostles' miracles and the drive of the New Testament pushes us towards Scripture as our authority rather than contemporary miracles backing up our words.

Jesus praises Thomas in John 20:29 for believing with all the evidence in front of him. He goes on to say that those who believe without seeing will be even more blessed. The miraculous in our day means nothing if we do not believe in the miracles of the Bible and, supremely, the resurrection. Just as one writer, John Woodhouse, says:

If the signs and wonders of the New Testament are not sufficiently wonderful for twenty-first century people, then we are not people of faith at all, but of rank unbelief.

Extra question – how else did they display Jesus' authority? (10:11-15)

The disciples are given the authority to pass judgment on the places they visit. The procedure of visiting a village is interesting. They are to look for those sympathetic to the gospel as a priority and to begin work from there.

10:11   'Worthy' means suitable and implies a person who is open to the apostles' message and willing to offer hospitality.

10:12-13   'Peace' was the standard greeting and conferred a blessing on the person receiving it. If that person has a wrong attitude they will not receive the 'peace'.

10:14   They are to be prepared for a complete rejection. 'To shake the dust off your feet' is an act of repudiation.

10:15   Those who oppose the gospel message will be judged even more severely than Sodom and Gomorrah, which were notoriously sinful cities (Genesis 18:20-21; 19:24-25).

Look at verses 9-10. Do you think that evangelism must be done without money and a change of clothes these days? What, then, do these verses imply about our possessions?

The mission was urgent and the apostles were to go just as they were, without making any special provision. They could trust God for their needs (see Matthew 6:25-33).

Whilst some people do try and 'live by faith' (and should be commended and aided) these verses probably apply to the disciples rather than us due to the immediate context of the commission to go to the lost sheep of Israel. However, it should get us thinking about possessions. The stuff we clutter our lives with may often stop us from finding time and energy for evangelism. Similarly, we are often too quick to add up what we have got and forget that everything we own is God's and may be a potential resource for his work. We must hold nothing back.

Application:

Where does our authority for evangelism come from? Do we have confidence that God's word in the Bible can change people? Why or why not?

If we are confident in the Bible, how should that affect our conversations with friends, in school, etc?

Verse 16 mentions four animals to help build up the picture of being one of Jesus' ambassadors. What are they and what do you think they mean?

The first pair of animals highlights the relationship between the Christian and the world. Sheep in the midst of wolves are in constant danger and depend solely on the shepherd for their defence and protection.

The second pair of animals indicates how Christians are therefore to act. They are not to be naive, but sensible and prudent like the serpent. 'Innocent' means pure and transparent.

Read verses 17-39. 42

These verses contain warnings of the conflict and persecution that Jesus' messengers should expect.

Jesus warns his disciples to expect opposition. From where does he say it will come? (10:17-21)

10:17   The religious authorities. Flogging in the synagogue was a punishment for disobedience or breaking the peace, perhaps by speaking an unpopular message.

10:18-20   The secular authorities. This verse refers to Gentiles as well as Jews, so is wider than the mission of vv. 5-6. The messengers would act as witnesses when explaining what they believed at their trial.

10:21   Family members.

10:22   General rejection.

How should the Christian live in the light of this? (10:19-31)

10:19-20   Do not worry about it in advance. It is natural to be afraid, but we can trust God to give us the words we need when being cross-questioned by the authorities.

10:22   Don't give up.

10:23   Move on when opposed (cf. v.14).
           'The Son of Man' is a title Jesus often used to refer to himself and it comes from Daniel 7:13-14, a recognised reference to the Messiah. In the Daniel verses the Son of Man comes to God to receive authority, glory and sovereign power. This verse, therefore, probably looks forward to Jesus' ascension (cf. Matthew 28:18) rather than to his second coming.

10:24-25   Don't be surprised when opposition comes. We should expect to share Jesus' unpopularity. The Pharisees said that Jesus' power to perform miracles came from Beelzebub (12:24,27).

10:26-28   Don't be afraid. The disciples had a duty to witness to the truth of what they had heard from Jesus and seen him do and this duty was to override their natural fear of the consequences.

10:29-31   Trust God for the future. Jesus' followers will not be immune from suffering and death (the sparrows still die), but nothing can happen outside God's control.

What does Jesus require from his followers? (10:32-33) What are the consequences?

Jesus' followers had to make a choice, whether or not to acknowledge him, and the consequences were eternal. It would be worth discussing whether keeping quiet about our relationship with Jesus is akin to disowning him before men.

The young people need to understand that we are only acceptable to God through our relationship with the Lord Jesus Christ.

How does the gospel affect our relationship with our family?

This is an important question to deal with since some young people might feel confused or threatened by what this chapter has to say about family. It is clear that families will be divided by the gospel (v. 21, 34-36). This might be the experience of some in the group and you might want to talk about that and support them in prayer now.

10:34	The Jews expected God's promised King to bring peace on earth (Isaiah 9:5-7, Zechariah 9:9-10) and understood this to mean absence of war, whereas the peace Jesus brought was a restored relationship with God. 

10:35-36   See Micah 7:6. The result of Jesus' mission will be divided families, as some members accept him as their King and others don't.

10:37   A huge challenge with respect to our relationship with our families. The verses seem to say that we must give them up for the gospel. This is not quite true – think of how many Christian families there are in your church. These verses really challenge our priorities when it comes to the gospel. Jesus must be number one on our priority list and so often he isn't. Each of us faces a different challenge to Jesus' authority over our lives and for some people it is family.

10:38-39   As Christians we 'take our cross' – literally meaning, we line up behind Jesus as 'cross-bearers', ready to put the gospel first in every way. Our old way of life is 'crucified with Christ' as Paul puts it in Galatians (2 v. 20 and 5 v. 24). The way of the King now becomes our overriding priority.

What is the privilege of following Jesus? (10:40-42)

10:40   Being identified with Jesus. Note also that the test of a person's relationship with Jesus was in the way his apostles were received.

10:41   An assurance of reward for those who accept the apostles' message.

10:42   Giving a cup of cold water was an essential act of hospitality and not deserving of a reward, so God's rewards go beyond what we deserve. The 'little ones' refer to Jesus' disciples, not to small children. The disciples shared the lowly status of children.

Prayer time.

Service? Songs.

Ali & Chris

PLANNING THE SESSION

Welcome

- Introduce yourselves.
- Start the meeting with prayer.

Getting to Know You

Split the group into pairs and ask them to talk about the weather, their pets or the programme they watched on television last night. Then ask everybody to report back something new about their partner to the rest of the group.

Most of us find it very easy to talk about inane subjects but hard to talk about the gospel. This session is all about making gospel-talk more frequent in our lives.

Talk Time

What was the last outstanding advert you saw? What was the slogan and the message the ad-men were putting across? How much should we believe about the claims they make, both visual and verbal?

'Ad-men' are shrewd and calculating. It is their job to seduce you into thinking you need their product. They use all sorts of methods: attractive imagery, catchy music, amusing slogans. As Christians we are not tasked with 'selling' the gospel, but we do have a message to get to people. We don't use deception, rather, we set forth the truth plainly (2 Corinthians 4 v. 2-3).

Focus Time

Divide the group into pairs and give each pair a torch. Split up to each end of the room and race to get a message from one person to the other using Morse Code. Morse is readily available on the internet. For added excitement turn the lights off so that it is difficult to spot which torch is your partner's. Don't make the message too long, remember that Morse is fairly slow for those unused to it.

You could play any game that involves getting a message from one person to another. Tongue twisters make good messages to pass on and the simplest game would be having everyone try to shout a different tongue twister to their partner at the same time.

Bible Time

See the worksheets on pages 86-87 for the Bible Study questions and running order. Photocopy these pages for each group member for use during the study.

This is a long study, so you might need to decide in advance which questions to concentrate on.

Prayer Time

A number of different issues might arise for prayer. The group might want to pray for encouragement and opportunities for evangelism, or for a particular evangelistic event that is coming up. Some people might have tried to talk about the gospel and experienced opposition. Be sensitive to these needs and share them with God.

You might also want to pray for missionaries and Christians around the world facing opposition and even violence and death for the sake of the gospel. You can find out more from your church's missionary committee or Patrick Johnstone's book *Operation World*.

Praise Time

Sing some songs that rehearse the gospel. Even singing the right stuff can help us remember it. For example, you could sing

'Lord, I lift your name on high' which contains the essence of the gospel story in the chorus. Another song that does this is 'In Christ Alone'.

For those groups who don't sing, read and think about a passage from the Bible that summarises the gospel message, e.g. Romans 3:21-26 or Titus 3:3-7

Extra Ideas

It is a good idea to be able to present the gospel clearly and concisely. Some people call it a 'napkin presentation' so you could use real napkins. First, let the group have a go at putting the elements of the gospel together. They can use pictures or words or both. Later in the exercise you may want to introduce a pre-written presentation, such as *Two Ways To Live*. (www.matthiasmedia.com.au/2wtl)

A further challenge could be to learn the gospel outline in this session or over successive weeks.

LESSON 4

THE HIDDEN KINGDOM

BIBLE READING

Matthew Chapter 13

TEACHING POINT

Jesus teaches about the nature of God's Kingdom through parables – the Kingdom of heaven has arrived and it is growing.

LEADER'S PREPARATION

In this third big teaching section of Matthew's gospel Jesus expands on what the Kingdom of heaven is like. The Kingdom has been preached and demonstrated for a while but there is growing opposition to Jesus' teaching and uncertainty about his identity. Chapter 11 records John the Baptist sending his disciples to Jesus to ask if he is the expected Messiah (11:2-6) and chapter 12 details opposition from the Pharisees (12:1-14, 22-37).

Jesus uses the first 'Kingdom parable' to challenge his listeners (and us) – how will you receive the message of the Kingdom? Through six further parables, some preached to the crowd, some told to the disciples, he further expounds the nature of the Kingdom.

Jesus teaches in parables on purpose. It was prophesied that he would do so (13:34-35 and Psalm 78:2), so Jesus is fulfilling prophecy. The reason for the parables is explained in verses 10-17. It is not to make things clearer, parables are not allegories. Although some things in the stories have clear parallels, as Jesus' explanation of the Sower shows, we are wrong to try to 'decode' them.

Parables often have a simple yet hard-hitting meaning, but one which is hidden. The meaning is hidden, as Jesus himself says, to force people to work at it. Those who want to know more will reap the rewards, but those who are satisfied just with the entertaining story will not be rewarded (13:12). There will always be people who close their ears to the truths about God's Kingdom (13:14-15). Apathy, inertia and other worries crowd out the message, as we shall see in the Parable of the Sower.

The remaining six parables consist of three pairs. The first and last teach about the separation of righteous people from the wicked on Judgment Day. The second and third teach about the imperceptible yet unstoppable growth of the Kingdom of heaven. The fourth and fifth are about the comparative value of the Kingdom.

So when the Kingdom was in its early stages and it was easy to doubt both the power and the significance of it, these parables helped the disciples (and help us) to see both. Additionally, there is a warning about ignoring the Kingdom. You cannot do that forever. Just as with the Sermon on the Mount (6:24-27) and the teaching about mission (10:28, 32-33), there is an element of the end times in this teaching section (theologians call it eschatology).

Read 13:1-9, 18-23 and fill in the table below:

Seeds fall on:	What happened?	Result:
Path	Eaten by birds	No crop
Rocky places	Quick growth but short-lived	No crop
Among thorns	Growth eventually choked	No crop
Good soil	Good growth	Crop – 100x, 60x, 30x

QUESTIONS
How many of the soils produce a crop? Why is this a surprise?

There is only one soil that produces a crop and there are only two outcomes. This is a bit of a surprise since we normally visualise four different outcomes. This should refine our understanding of the Kingdom – people are in or out. No half way.

Jesus himself gives us the meaning of the parable. Most importantly what is the sowing of the seed? (v.19) Look back at 10:7. What activity that we are engaged in is this parable talking about?

The sowing of the seed is hearing 'the message of the Kingdom'. This is the message that the disciples were charged with delivering in Matthew 10. So it is akin to our evangelism too.

What are the different reasons for there being no crop in Jesus' explanation?

1.   The evil one comes and snatches the 'seed' before someone can understand it.
2.   Receiving it with joy, but giving up as soon as persecution or trouble comes along.
3.   Giving it a go, but struggling with life's worries and, particularly, wealth.

In what ways these days does the message of the Kingdom get lost, choked or withered?

For an ancient story it contains timeless realities. The things that stopped people responding to the gospel in the first century are really the same today. Some people reject it out of hand, others try it for a while until they are under pressure, then it all comes unstuck. Finally, people are drawn back to the world, often by wealth, and give up on the gospel. You might want to talk about some specific issues with the group, e.g. time, the pressure of getting a good education, peer pressure, etc.

How is this parable a warning and an encouragement for evangelism?

This parable warns us that evangelism is tough. Three of the four soils were unproductive. Some that seemed to be going so well just fade away. This is inevitably our experience too. However there is a soil that yields a crop and that's the encouragement. Our modern farming methods that can put seeds in very exact places mean we have lost the picture of the farmer spreading the seed by hand, but farmers did that because they knew that there would be a crop alongside all the seed that was lost. So we evangelise where we can because God will honour his word and it will not return to him empty (Isaiah 55:10-11).

The Weeds and the Net – read verses 24-30 and 47-52. What are the similarities between the two parables? What do these similarities emphasise?

- a mixture of desirable and undesirable things, wheat/weeds, good fish/bad fish
- a harvest and gathering in
- a subsequent division – wheat from weeds, good from bad fish
- destruction – of the weeds and bad fish.

The similarities emphasise the 'now and not yet' of God's Kingdom. Citizens of God's Kingdom presently rub shoulders with non-citizens (v.38) while the full inauguration of the Kingdom is delayed, but it will not always be that way. There will be a final day and a judgment when good will be divided from bad and the bad will be destroyed.

Why should we be both encouraged and warned?

The emphasis seems to be on warning about the end times. This is an encouragement for Christians living in the world that seems to be so opposed to Christianity. It won't stay this way for ever. But it is a warning to make a decision to accept Jesus' kingly rule and live for the Saviour before the time of dividing (see study 6).

The Mustard Seed and the Yeast – read verses 31-35. In spite of all the problems the Kingdom of God faces, what encouragement do these parables give?

It often seems that the gospel does not make a difference in people's lives or that the church is ignored or laughed at.

However this parable reminds us that, whatever the outward perception, God's Kingdom is present and it is growing. You don't see a tiny seed begin to grow, you cannot see what yeast does in the dough. However, the eventual effects are obvious – a large plant and bread that has risen.

How did Jesus' life itself have a huge impact from small beginnings?

Jesus is rejected more often than not in the gospels. Eventually the authorities try to snuff out Christianity by putting him to death. And yet from this seemingly foolish start (1 Corinthians 1:18ff) comes a worldwide faith and the start of the eternal Kingdom of heaven. The disciples too are not really a promising bunch at first and yet, with God's help and the Holy Spirit, they achieve great things for the gospel.

Are there small 'mustard seed' changes you could make in your life that will begin to have a big effect? Are there small things you could do as you talk to your friends about Jesus that will have a knock-on effect?

This is a bit of a 'cheesy' way of putting it, but we so often back down on the problems we have in discipleship and evangelism because everything seems too hard or too big. It is true that most of our growth as Christians will be incremental and that God will honour even our small attempts to talk to our friends about the gospel.

The Hidden Treasure and the Pearl – read verses 44-45. In each case what did the men in the story do to receive his treasure?

In both stories the men sell everything. The treasure they are after (treasure trove or fine pearl) is worth absolutely everything to them.

What should this tell us about the Kingdom of heaven?

It tells us, very simply, that it is worth all that we have got. It is truly valuable beyond everything in this world and worth giving up everything for. We are reminded of Matthew 10:37-39.

What are you prepared to give up to go on being a Christian?

How seriously do you take all this Christianity stuff? That's really what this parable is asking. Here are two men who gave up everything because they knew the value of what they sought. Is being a Christian really just a hobby? Or a good place to meet with friends?

Look up Philippians 3:7-11. What was Paul's perspective? Put verse 8 into your own words:

This is an interesting verse that we have watered down. The word for 'rubbish' is literally 'dung'. Paul's reaction to anything other than 'knowing Christ' is the same as if we have stepped in something unsavoury on the pavement. Keep this gem back until the group have written their sentences unless you want some very interesting answers!

Bishop Ryle said (quite a long time ago!) 'If a man is truly convinced of the importance of the Kingdom, if he is truly convinced of the importance of salvation, he will give up everything to win Christ and eternal life.' Now is a great time to challenge the group about whether they are truly convinced that knowing God's love and salvation is the most valuable thing it is possible to have in this life.

PLANNING THE SESSION

Welcome

- Introduce yourselves.
- Start the meeting with prayer.

Getting to Know You

Give everybody a piece of paper and tell them to write down five words that summarise their lives, e.g. Born. Drooled. Played. Exams. Relax. Tell them that they are trying to summarise the story of their life in these five words. Either share with one another, or keep them anonymous, mix them up and have everyone try to guess each other's.

If this doesn't work you could try to summarise a fairy tale (or other books) in only five words, e.g. Stepsisters, Ball, Godmother, Slipper, Wedding = Cinderella.

Talk Time

Talk about why we identify with stories so well. Why are soap operas popular amongst some people? Why do we find it easier to remember things told as stories rather than listed in bullet point format?

There are all sorts of answers to this ranging from our identifying with characters in the story to the need for escapism, which is stronger in some than others. This introduces the idea of stories and parables which dominate Matthew chapter 13.

Focus Time

Play a game that involves telling stories. This could be a 'Shaggy Dog' story with each person getting a word, a sentence or a certain amount of time each. Or you could bring in some random objects and divide the group into teams to make up stories based on the same objects.

Bible Time

See the worksheets on pages 88-89 for the Bible Study questions and running order. Photocopy these pages for each group member for use during the study.

Prayer Time

Pray for yourselves that God will help you to trust Him when it seems that the Kingdom is not growing sometimes. Pray for help in arranging our own priorities around the true value of God's Kingdom.

Pray for friends that they will respond to the call of God's Kingdom before it is too late.

Praise Time

Sing 'All that I am I lay before you' or 'Be thou my vision'. Both these songs reflect a desire to put God's Kingdom first in all things. Verse 4 of 'Be thou my vision' particularly matches the parables of the Hidden Treasure and the Pearl. If you don't want to sing you could read the words aloud whilst people think of things that they treasure (riches or 'man's empty praise' – we might value status rather than material things) and how incomparable they are to God's eternal Kingdom.

Extra Ideas

Make a collage, or a Powerpoint presentation of things that we treasure in this world so that you can talk about the relative value of these things. You could use appropriate music to play with the Powerpoint presentation.

LESSON 5

KiNGDOM RELATIONSHIPS

BIBLE READING

Matthew Chapter 18

TEACHING POINT

Humility is the hallmark of God's new Kingdom.

LEADER'S PREPARATION

Chapter 18 follows on from Peter's confession of Jesus being the Christ (16:13-20), Jesus teaching the disciples about his forthcoming death and resurrection (16:21-28) and the Transfiguration (17:1-13). Chapter 18 starts with the disciples, having recognised Jesus as God's promised King, questioning him about who would be the greatest in the heavenly Kingdom.

By now we are familiar with the idea of the Kingdom of heaven. All three of the previous teaching blocks in Matthew have given us more details. It would be very easy to become complacent and a little smug about it. Unfortunately, this sometimes happens in churches. Christians begin to look down on one another, divisions and pecking orders emerge and the church begins to look more and more like the world around it.

Jesus' fourth discourse in chapter 18 acts as a corrective to that and hinges around the idea of the 'little child' (18:2). We often use the picture in verses 2-4 to endorse our children's work within church. Certainly, children's and youth work is of utmost importance and our attitude towards young people must be different from that of Jesus' day. In first century Judea children were of no importance, they had no power or influence and were merely to be looked after until they became adults. For Jesus to instruct his disciples to become like little children and welcome them would have been an alien concept.

However, we need to push the idea further in this study because it is not merely about children. The humility and dependence of a child was what the disciples were to emulate. So a Christian living in God's Kingdom is one in whom these traits are strong. It is very often new Christians who get it right. Because accepting Christ's death and trusting in him means acknowledging our own helplessness, we are most 'childlike' when we have recently been converted. It is only later that we begin to think we are 'grown-up' Christians and that we can do things in our own strength.

Jesus highlights some of the worst ways we can behave towards our Christian brothers and sisters. We can cause them to stumble (18:6); look down on them (18:10); and hold grudges (18:21). The concepts in this chapter are quite complex and there are some tricky verses to understand (e.g. 18:8-10), but pray for some big changes and radically new attitudes within the group.

How does Jesus turn the disciples' question in verse 1 on its head? What does Jesus mean when he says 'like little children'? (18:2-4)

Jesus takes someone of no importance and little prestige and says that they are an example of the 'greatest' in the Kingdom of heaven. Even more shockingly, Jesus says that the disciples have to change to be like the child in order to enter the Kingdom.

The link between humility and the child helps us understand the meaning. A child is someone who is totally dependent on others for food, safety, etc. Also, they know instinctively that they are 'small' (not necessarily physically) rather than great. It is this dependence and lack of status that are key characteristics for becoming a Christian. We have to acknowledge that we are 'not great', in God's view we are sinful. We have to concede that we can do nothing for ourselves and totally depend on God for our salvation.

What false impression do the disciples have about God's Kingdom?

Their mistake is to think of it as a hierarchy and the more mature you are as a Christian the more important you become. Jesus wants them (and us) to realise that we have to continue humbly in the Kingdom, just as we entered it in the first place.

Verses 5-14 teach us more about God's perspective on relationships in the Kingdom. How should we treat our fellow Christians?

18:5   As equals. 'In Jesus' name' means for his sake, submitting to his authority and recognising our status as being like a little child. All believers are equally dependent on God for every need, spiritual as well as physical.

18:6   Don't do anything that will cause another believer to sin (or stumble). Note how seriously Jesus views this offence.

How easy is it to feel part of the group? Do newcomers feel welcome?

18:7-9   Treat sin seriously, especially our own. Is there anything in my life that causes offence to others?

The dealing with sin aspect is tricky and may need sensitivity. However, the meaning of Jesus' phrase is clear. The hand-chopping and eye-gouging tells us that our response to sin needs to be both rigorous and irreversible. Clearly there are not thousands of Christians wandering around who have physically done these things. Talk about what the picture of both the severity of and permanent dealing with sin means for the group.

18:10   Don't look down on other Christians.

This verse talks about the angels of these 'little ones' (believers) seeing the face of the Father in heaven. People have differing views on what this means. Some use it as a proof text for the existence of guardian angels – a supposed angel/person who looks after us in particular. However, this is the only verse in the Bible that seems to support this. Others think that the 'angels' are the spirits of believers, who are continuously in the presence of God. In Acts 12:15

the members of Jerusalem church thought that Rhoda had answered the door to Peter's angel.

In our culture there is much interest in angels, vampires, werewolves and other supernatural beings. Don't get sidetracked into spending a lot of time on the issue of guardian angels. The important thing to note is that each believer (little one) is precious to God, as the following parable shows.

18:12-14   Care for those who are in danger of falling away. All believers are precious to God and we need to be aware of those who are on the fringe and take positive steps to include them.

How might we fall into the traps and end up doing what we shouldn't?

There will be lots of different answers to this question of application. It somewhat depends on how long the group members have been Christians. Complacency is one way we begin to develop bad habits ourselves. We also might become casual or neglectful about certain sins. When these attitudes are around within the group it is easy for those who have been Christians for less time to be drawn into bad and sinful habits. It is also possible that more experienced Christians may belittle those who are trying to live as the Bible demands with the enthusiasm that comes soon after conversion.

What steps can we take to make sure we do what we should?

This answer should be a good discussion as well. Note that the things we are challenged to do are the antidote to looking down on others and causing them to stumble.

In the light of the above, look at what is happening in your group. Is there anything that should be changed? How can you make sure that everyone feels included?

How should we manage situations where there is a major disagreement between group members? (18:15-20)

We need to challenge our group members about not bearing grudges and being willing to forgive. In a situation with another Christian where there are two possible interpretations, encourage them to assume that hurt is not intended.

18:15   The aim is always to win your brother over and this should be at the forefront of our thinking.
         Firstly, go and discuss it privately, without having talked to other people about it. This prevents gossip and talking behind people's backs, both of which cause rifts in relationships within a group.

18:16   If that fails, take two or three witnesses.

18:17   If the situation remains unresolved, the matter should be aired before the whole group.

18:18-20 You may decide not to cover these verses.

18:18   'You' is plural and refers to the disciples, not just to Peter (16:19). The church is able to declare what is accepted and what is not on the basis of Jesus' teaching.

18:19-20 When looked at in context this is not a reference to corporate prayer. The phrase translated 'anything you ask for' can mean 'any judicial matter', i.e. any matter under dispute, referring back to the previous verses.

Living this way is not going to be easy (18:21). How does the Parable of the Unmerciful Servant help? (18:23-35)

18:21   The scribes said that one must forgive three times, so Peter thought he was being generous.

18:22   The number Jesus gives is too large to keep track of. Jesus is saying that an attitude of forgiveness must be a Christian's lifestyle.

18:23-35   We, like the first servant, have been forgiven a colossal debt. Any debt owed to us by others is miniscule by comparison. When we remember what God has forgiven us, how can we not forgive our Christian brothers and sisters when they offend us?

Welcome

- Introduce yourselves.
- Start the meeting with prayer.

Getting to Know You

Do an exercise in building others up, since that is what we are called on to do for one another. Each person's name can be written on a card (perhaps like a birthday card). If you can get photographs of the group in advance to turn into cards even better. (You would have to be organised with the digital camera on the previous week.) Display the cards or pass them round the group. Each person can anonymously write one or two good things about each person in the card. The cards can then be read by each member, or put in envelopes and posted to arrive later in the week.

Talk Time

Divide the group into pairs and ask them to tell each other about the best present they have ever had and who it was from. Share with the larger group. Discuss why we give presents and what this says about our feelings for the recipients. We give good gifts to those we love. Today we are going to see what Jesus said about the way we should treat each other.

Focus Time

Humility is little understood these days and often mistaken for just being wishy-washy. Divide the group into threes or fours and get them to draw a spider diagram with 'Humility' at the centre and branches for everything they can think of about it. Be prepared with some ideas of your own, because some groups might struggle to get many ideas.

Bible Time

See the worksheets on pages 90-91 for the Bible Study questions and running order. Photocopy these pages for each group member for use during the study.

Prayer Time

Take some time to pray for one another in the group. If the group feel comfortable enough to share difficulties they might have being humble, let them. (You might want to split into small groups for this session). Pray too for less regular members of the group that they will be welcomed and encouraged when they attend and not feel excluded.

Praise Time
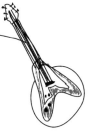
Sing some songs together that remind you of the greatness of God and our need to be humble. For example, the chorus 'Overwhelmed by love' or the hymn 'Great is your faithfulness'

   If you don't want to sing read Philippians 2:5-11 together to praise God for Jesus' humility and the salvation he brings.

Extra Ideas

Use blindfolds and have pairs guide one another through an obstacle course. The object is to not let your partner stumble.

LESSON 6

THY KINGDOM COME

BIBLE READING

Matthew Chapters 24-25.

TEACHING POINT

What will happen when the Kingdom of heaven comes in reality and how should we prepare for it?

LEADER'S PREPARATION

The final two chapters we are looking at are 24 and 25 – the signs of the end of the age. But, once again, before we get there we must not overlook the chapters in between. Matthew does not pad out his gospel, it's all there for a reason. Chapters 19-23 revolve around the confrontations that Jesus meets in his ministry, most of which are with the religious leaders. Throughout these chapters we see them refusing to acknowledge Jesus as the Christ, God's promised King. Following his denunciation of the Pharisees and teachers of the Law for their hypocrisy and wickedness (23:1-36), Jesus leaves Jerusalem with his disciples (24:1).

Chapters 24-25 are one speech made by Jesus to his disciples in response to their question in 24:3 (note the two bookends in 24:3 and 26:1). Jesus has predicted, somewhat enigmatically, that the magnificent temple buildings will be thrown down to the last stone (v.2) and his disciples, naturally enough, want to know when and how.

QUESTIONS

What did the disciples ask Jesus? (24:3)

Jesus is sitting on the Mount of Olives, which has a view over the whole of Jerusalem.

The question consists of two parts: when will the temple be destroyed? and, what will be the sign of Jesus' return and of the end of the age? (The end of the age refers to the final judgment – see 13:39).

Jesus' answer deals with both parts of the question and it is not always easy to tell them apart. Chapter 24:15-20 deal with the events leading up to the destruction of the temple.

What are some of the signs of the last days that Jesus talks about? (24:4-12)

The last days comprise the whole of the period between Jesus' first and second comings.

24:5   False Christs will arise who will deceive many (see also vv.23-26). Many will claim to have found the 'real' Christ. Don't listen to them, says Jesus. The real second coming will be unmistakable.

24:6-7   Wars and rumours of wars. The world will be in turmoil. You could talk about how we see this in the newspapers. Our world has always been like this since Jesus' time. A world without God tends towards this chaos.

24:7   Famines and earthquakes in various places.

24:9-10   Persecution of Christians, causing many to fall away. The word used for 'be persecuted' is the same as for 'distress' in verses 21 and 29. This is becoming increasingly relevant in our culture.
People will turn away from faith in these last days. Do the young people think this is particularly true of their generation?

24:11   Deceivers, false prophets and 'anti-Christs' will appear. Don't get bogged down in the details, the group mustn't get a 'reds under the bed' syndrome. However, we are warned that Christians and Christianity will face some powerful and personal enmity.

24:12   General wickedness will increase.

Jesus does give his followers much to be encouraged by in the midst of the doom and gloom. Can you spot the encouragements? (24:13-35)

24:13   We must stand firm and not be swayed by what is happening in the world around us. God honours those who honour him and is faithful to his promise to save.

24:14	The end is in God's hands and the gospel will go out into all the world.
24:22	God will cut short the days of suffering for the sake of the elect (his chosen people i.e. Christians).
24:25	We have been warned. This is not a surprise, God wants us to be ready.
24:30	Jesus will return in glory and unmistakably.
24:31	God will gather his people home, wherever and whoever they are.
24:35	Whatever happens to the world, God's promises will still stand firm.

Being Ready

The second section (24:36 – 25:46) gives us a number of different pictures that increasingly reveal what it means to be prepared for Jesus' return. We are taught that Jesus' return is inevitable, but may be long delayed; will be sudden but cannot be predicted, and that it will come with terrible consequences for those who are not ready.

There is a lot packed into the end of chapter 24 and chapter 25. Five parables and stories tell us four different things about waiting for Jesus' return.

Read 24:36-41. To what is Jesus' return compared? What do we learn about Jesus' return and what must we do?

Jesus' return is compared to the time of Noah. At that time people did not expect the flood, it came as a big surprise. So it will be for people when Jesus returns. But Christians must not be surprised because we know that his return is inevitable, even if we do not know when it will be.

The implication is that Christians must live expecting the return at any time. For us it is not a surprise.

Read 24:42-44. To what is Jesus' return likened? What do we learn about Jesus' return and what must we do?

Jesus' return is likened to the coming of a thief to rob a house. We learn that the time of Jesus' return is unknown. If you knew your house was about to be robbed you would stay up to stop it happening. You would be prepared.

So we must be prepared. The warning that Jesus will return at an unspecified date is similar to a warning about a thief who will rob you. You could talk about what sort of things we need to do to be prepared – making sure of your salvation through Christ, maintaining a relationship with Jesus, telling others, etc.

Read 24:45-51. What is the attitude of the wicked servant?
What do we learn about Jesus' return and how are we to be wise servants?

The wicked servant assumes that the master will be away for a long time, perhaps indefinitely (v.48). He does not expect the master to return (v.50). He therefore lives as if the master is not returning by oppressing others and 'eating and drinking with drunkards'.

Through this we learn that Jesus' return is certain and we shouldn't ignore the fact that it will happen. This parable also builds on the previous one by once again emphasising the unknown aspect of the timing of Jesus' return.

We are, therefore, to be wise as we wait for Jesus' return. This means we are not to act like the wicked servant by indulging in licentiousness and oppression of others. In particular the attitude between servants seems to be highlighted, i.e. the relationship between Christians, not that we are free to behave badly to those outside the Kingdom.

Note, finally, that this parable introduces a warning (v.51), which is picked up in all the following parables in chapter 25. The idea is not to scare people into the Kingdom, but to make sure that the consequences of not being ready are crystal clear.

Read 25:1-13. What was wrong with the foolish girls' behaviour?
What do we learn about Jesus' return and how do we avoid being careless and lazy whilst we wait?

The foolish girls were not prepared because they, like the wicked servant, were not expecting the bridegroom's arrival. They knew he would return (there would be no wedding otherwise!), but not when. Rather than resulting in wicked behaviour their foolishness revealed itself in laziness and thoughtlessness. They assumed that there would be enough time to prepare themselves once the groom returned.

Again, this parable builds on the previous ones. Jesus' return is certain, but the timing is unknown and he will return unexpectedly. Note, once more, the consequences of not being ready – being shut out (v.10). Being cut off from God is a key theme of punishments throughout the Bible.

We can avoid being careless and lazy by not giving into complacency. It is very easy to slip into a familiar groove of lifestyle, not allowing ourselves to be challenged. What challenges should we not avoid in our walk with Christ? To have a conversation with a non-Christian friend, and not duck it? To find time for a quiet time even if it means personal sacrifice, such as getting up earlier?

The potentially long delay means that we have to plan. We cannot just live as if Jesus will return next week. We have to assume that he may not and plan to tell others, raise leaders and teach the next generation God's praiseworthy deeds (Psalm 78:4).

Read 25:14-30. How is the loyalty of the servants tested?
What view of the master does each servant take?
How should the church cope positively with the delay?

The loyalty of the servants is tested by the length of time that the master is away. It seems (again) that he will not return or will be a long, long time. His imminent return is totally unexpected. The character of the servants during a long wait is being examined.

Two servants realise that they must improve upon what the master has given them. They see the delay as an opportunity to do their best for the master. They see the positive side of the master, that he expects and rewards hard work. It is worth noting that the word 'servant' is really 'slave' (doulos in Greek). For a slave work is not an option but a requirement. A talent is a weight, usually of silver, of enormous value – not necessarily talent/abilities as we sometimes interpret this parable. We are naturally in possession of the priceless treasure of God's Kingdom. As slaves it is our duty to work as these two servants did.

The third servant has a different attitude. He has a lopsided view of the master (God) believing him to be a tough, ruthless employer. God is certainly tough and jealous, but this ignores the loving and righteous side of God's character. The third servant acts in his own self-interest not to take risks and to guard his treasure jealously. His selfishness is punished.

The church and Christians should therefore take heed and not bury their heads in the sand. This parable is about growing God's valuable Kingdom – taking the assets that God has left us with, including the good news of the gospel, and growing them into more. This may involve using our personal skills and talents, but there is a wider aspect too.

Read 25:31-46. What is the difference between the sheep and the goats?

The sheep love Jesus (the Good Shepherd) and his flock (v.34-40).

25:34　　The Kingdom (final destiny of the sheep) was prepared for them since the creation of the world, so must be due to grace, not works. Scripture teaches that our salvation is through faith alone (Romans 3:21-24), but saving faith is always accompanied by works, the fruit of faith (James 2:14-26).

25:35-36　　The reason for the decision of verse 34 is their attitude to the King.

25:40　　The brothers of Jesus are the believers (cf. 12:49-50). So in verse 45 'the least of these' also refers to believers.

They have different destinations (v. 34 and v. 41 and 46).

How should we behave in the light of verses 31-46?

Discuss practical ways to encourage your group to both care for their fellow Christians and evangelise their non-Christian friends.

PLANNING THE SESSION

Welcome

- Introduce yourselves.
- Start the meeting with prayer.

Getting to Know You

Play a game which requires a little prediction. Something like 'Play your cards right', guessing whether a sequence of hidden cards are higher or lower than the previous. This should just be treated as a bit of fun, but it highlights how impossible it is to know the future and leads into the Talk Time.

Talk Time

What would you really like to know about the future? Why do you think it fascinates us?

Answers will probably revolve around next week's lottery results and what questions will be in the upcoming exam. The point is that we are simultaneously worried and fascinated by the future. We are in thrall to it because the future is unknown and may have consequences for us. We want to try and control it.

Focus Time

Play a game that involves planning for different occasions. Choose an event (e.g. an earthquake, shipwreck, party or foreign holiday). Give the groups about one minute to write down a list of equipment they would take in a suitcase or survival kit. You could either decide in advance what items will win points, or accept anything that the group can reasonably argue the case for (be strict). Award two points if only one group has the item or one point if two or more groups have it on the list. If you have time play several rounds.

Bible Time

See the worksheets on pages 92-93 for the Bible Study questions and running order. Photocopy these pages for each group member for use during the study.

Prayer Time

Pray that God will help you not to be complacent about the future and that he will give you the strength in order to prepare well for Jesus' return. Think about some friends to pray for. Pray that they will get to know Jesus before it is too late and that they, too, will begin to live with the urgency that comes from knowing Jesus could return at any time.

Praise Time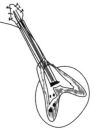

You could sing together, focussing on songs that are about Jesus' return and our commitment to him, such as 'These are the days of Elijah' or 'O, Jesus I have promised'.

   If you don't want to sing you could read 1 Thessalonians 4:13 – 5:11 together and spend some time responding in prayer.

Extra Ideas

Play a game that involves division. For example, 'Animal sounds' where the group divides into sub-groups based on animal noises. You could start with sheep and goats for example.

INTRODUCING THE KING (Matthew 1–4)

THE KINGDOM OF HEAVEN WORKSHEET

Part 1 – An Overview of Matthew's Gospel

Look at Matthew 1:1-17. Can you see any names you recognise? Why does Matthew want us to associate the birth of Jesus (1:18 onwards) with some of these names?

Look up 7:28; 11:1; 13:53; 19:1; 26:1. What similarities are there between the verses? What does each verse conclude? Why do you think we get this repetition?

Look up 4:17 and 23 and 9:35. What is Jesus described as doing? What word is repeated in each verse and what do you think it means?

Part 2 – Jesus is God's Promised King

Look at 1:18 – 2:23. How does Matthew show that Jesus came from God and is the one promised by the prophets?

Read Matthew 3:1-12. What was John preaching? (3:2) Who came to visit him and what did they do? (3:5-6)
Who is John not pleased to see? Why is he suspicious of these people? What does John warn of? (3:7-10)

How does John describe Jesus? (3:11-12) Why do you think he uses such strong language?

Read Matthew 4:17. What is Jesus' message?

Think. Are you ready to come face to face with Jesus? What do you need to repent of before God's Kingdom arrives in full? What do you think 'fruit in keeping with repentance' might mean for you?

THE KINGDOM OF HEAVEN WORKSHEET

Read Matthew 4:23-25.

What was Jesus doing?

How did this demonstrate that he is the promised King? (Isaiah 35:5-6; 61:1)

Read Matthew 5:1-12

What are the Christian characteristics described in these verses? What qualities does the world value rather than these?

Fill in the table:

Characteristic	Meaning	World's Values

What things stop me living this way? How does it help to know that God is a gracious God?

Read Matthew 5:13-16.
Believers are witnesses for the Kingdom (5:13-16). What two metaphors does Jesus use?

Read Matthew 5:17-20.

What does Jesus say about his relationship to the Old Testament? (5:17-18)

How do we relate to the Law? (5:19)

How can our righteousness surpass that of the Pharisees? (5:20)

Read Matthew 7:13-27

What are the four paired alternatives? What does each one teach about following the King?

How should our thinking be shaped by these exclusive claims in a culture of relativism and pluralism?

THE KINGDOM OF HEAVEN WORKSHEET

Read Matthew 9:35 – 10:1.

How does Matthew summarise Jesus' ministry so far? What authority does he give to his disciples?

Read Matthew 10:1-15.

What was their target group and what was the message? (10:5-7)

What tools were the disciples given to authenticate the message? (10:1, 8)

How else did they display Jesus' authority? (10:11-15)

Look at verses 9-10. Do you think that evangelism must be done without money and a change of clothes these days? What, then, do these verses imply about our possessions?

Application

Where does our authority for evangelism come from? Do we have confidence that God's word in the Bible can change people? Why or why not?

If we are confident in the Bible, how should that affect our conversations with friends, in school, etc?

Read Matthew 10:16

This verse mentions four animals to help build up the picture of being one of Jesus' ambassadors. What are they and what do you think they mean?

Read Matthew 10:17-39.

Jesus warns his disciples to expect opposition. From where does he say it will come? (10:17-21)

How should the Christian live in the light of this? (10:19-31)

What does Jesus require from his followers? (10:32-33) What are the consequences?

How does the gospel affect our relationship with our family?

Read Matthew 10:40-42.

What is the privilege of following Jesus?

THE KINGDOM OF HEAVEN WORKSHEET

Read Matthew 13:1-9, 18-23 and fill in the table below:

Seeds fall on:	What happened?	Result:

How many of the soils produce a crop? Why is this a surprise?

Jesus himself gives us the meaning of the parable. Most importantly, what is the sowing of the seed? (v.19) Look back at 10:7. What activity that we are engaged in is this parable talking about?

What are the different reasons for there being no crop in Jesus' explanation?

In what ways these days does the message of the Kingdom get lost, choked or withered?

How is this parable a warning and an encouragement for evangelism?

The Weeds and the Net – read verses 24-30 and 47-52.

What are the similarities between the two parables? What do these similarities emphasise?

Why should we be both encouraged and warned?

The Mustard Seed and the Yeast – read verses 31-35.

In spite of all the problems the Kingdom of God faces, what encouragement do these parables give?

How did Jesus' life itself have a huge impact from small beginnings?

Are there small 'mustard seed' changes you could make in your life that will begin to have a big effect? Are there small things you could do as you talk to your friends about Jesus that will have a knock-on effect?

The Hidden Treasure and the Pearl – read verses 44-45.

In each case what did the men in the story do to receive his treasure?

What should this tell us about the Kingdom of heaven?

What are you prepared to give up to go on being a Christian?

Look up Philippians 3:7-11. What was Paul's perspective? Put verse 8 into your own words:

THE KINGDOM OF HEAVEN WORKSHEET

Read Matthew 18:1-4.

How does Jesus turn the disciples' question in verse 1 on its head? What does Jesus mean when he says 'like little children'? (18:2-4)

What false impression do the disciples have about God's Kingdom?

Read Matthew 18:5-14.

These verses teach us more about God's perspective on relationships in the Kingdom. How should we treat our fellow Christians?

How might we fall into the traps and end up doing what we shouldn't?

What steps can we take to make sure we do what we should?

Read Matthew 18:15-20.

How should we manage situations where there is a major disagreement between group members?

Living this way is not going to be easy (18:21). How does the Parable of the Unmerciful Servant help? (18:23-35)

Read Matthew 24:1-12.

What did the disciples ask Jesus? (24:3)

What are some of the signs of the last days that Jesus talks about? (24:4-12)

Read Matthew 24:13-35.

Jesus does give his followers much to be encouraged by in the midst of the doom and gloom. Can you spot the encouragements?

Being Ready

Matthew 24:36 – 25:46 gives us a number of different pictures showing us what it means to be prepared for Jesus' return.

Read Matthew 24:36-41.

To what is Jesus' return compared?
What do we learn about Jesus' return and what must we do?

Read Matthew 24:42-44.

To what is Jesus' return likened?
What do we learn about Jesus' return and what must we do?

Read Matthew 24:45-51.

What is the attitude of the wicked servant?
What do we learn about Jesus' return and how are we to be wise servants?

Read Matthew 25:1-13.

What was wrong with the foolish girls' behaviour?

What do we learn about Jesus' return and how do we avoid being careless and lazy whilst we wait?

Read Matthew 25:14-30.

How is the loyalty of the servants tested?

What view of the master does each servant take?

How should the church cope positively with the delay?

Read Matthew 25:31-46.

What is the difference between the sheep and the goats?

How should we behave in the light of verses 31-46?

The Kingdom of Heaven
Extra Lessons

If you decide to study the whole of Matthew's gospel the following order is suggested:

1. Introducing the King .... Matthew 1-4

An overview of Matthew's gospel and an introduction to Jesus, God's promised King.

2. Introducing the Kingdom .... Matthew 5-7

Jesus explains what life in the new Kingdom is like.

3. Signs of the King .... Matthew 7:28 – 9:34

Jesus demonstrates his authority as King – teaching, healing, forgiving sin, etc.

4. Proclaiming the Kingdom ...... Matthew 10:1-42

The training and warnings Jesus gives his disciples as they prepare to go and preach the good news of the Kingdom.

5. Opposition to the Kingdom .... Matthew 11-12

Jesus confirms his identity and denounces those who reject him.

6. The Hidden Kingdom .... Matthew 13:1-58

Examining the parables that unpack what the Kingdom of heaven is like.

7. Confessing the King .... Matthew 14-17

Jesus' hearers are increasingly polarised into two camps – those who accept Jesus as God's promised King and those who reject him.

8. Kingdom Relationships .... Matthew 18:1-35

Jesus teaches about right and wrong attitudes and relationships in the Kingdom of heaven.

9. Rejecting the King's Authority .... Matthew 19–23

Confrontations with the religious leaders, who refuse to acknowledge Jesus as God's promised King.

10. Thy Kingdom Come .... Matthew 24–25

What will happen when the Kingdom of heaven comes in reality and how we should prepare for that day.

11. The King of Salvation .... Matthew 26–28

The death, resurrection and ascension of Jesus and his commission to his disciples to take the message of the Kingdom to the whole world.

Christian Focus Publications publishes books for adults and children under its four main imprints: Christian Focus, Christian Heritage, CF4K and Mentor. Our books reflect that God's word is reliable and Jesus is the way to know him, and live for ever with him.

Our children's publication list includes a Sunday school curriculum that covers pre-school to early teens; puzzle and activity books. We also publish personal and family devotional titles, biographies and inspirational stories that children will love.

If you are looking for quality Bible teaching for children then we have an excellent range of Bible story and age specific theological books.

From pre-school to teenage fiction, we have it covered!

Find us at our web page:
www.christianfocus.com